BROADWAY
in the '90s

782.14 B7832 MAY 05 1999 WITHDRAW

Broadway in the '90s 16.95

FROM THE RECOR

MID CONTINENT PU

MID-CONTINENT PUBLIC LIBRARY

Riverside Branch **RS**
2700 N.W. Vivion Rd.
Riverside, MO 64150

D1294947

ISBN 0-7935-9526-6

HAL•LEONARD®
CORPORATION

7777 W. BLUEMOUND RD. P.O. BOX 13819 MILWAUKEE, WI 53213

For all works contained herein:
Unauthorized copying, arranging, adapting, recording or public performance is an infringement of copyright.

MID-CONTINENT PUBLIC LIBRARY

3 0000 11863909 9

MID-CONTINENT PUBLIC LIBRARY
Riverside Branch
2700 N.W. Vivion Rd.
Riverside, MO 64150

D RS

Contents

ALONE AT THE DRIVE-IN MOVIE
from GREASE

Lyric and Music by WARREN CASEY
and JIM JACOBS

© 1971, 1972 WARREN CASEY and JIM JACOBS
All Rights Controlled by EDWIN H. MORRIS & COMPANY, A Division of MPL Communications, Inc.
All Rights Reserved

at the pas - sion pit want-ing you.

Owoooo, owoooo   And when the in - ter-mis - sion elf   moves the

clock's hands, ___   When he's eat-ing ___ ev-'ry-thing   sold at the

stand,   When there's one   min-ute to go   'til the

lights go down low, I'll be hold-ing the speak - er knobs, miss-ing you

so._____ *rubato* I can't be - lieve_ it,_____ *a tempo*

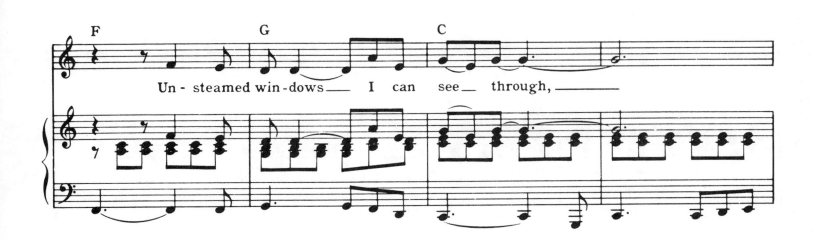

Un - steamed win-dows_ I can see_ through,_____

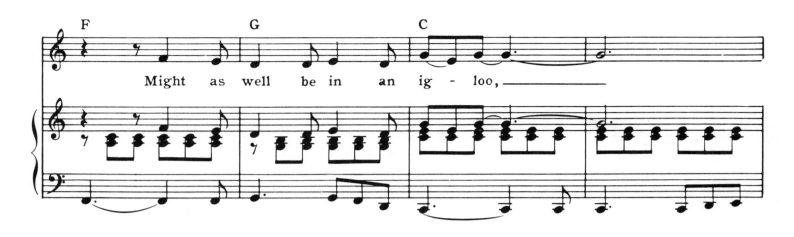

Might as well be in an ig - loo,

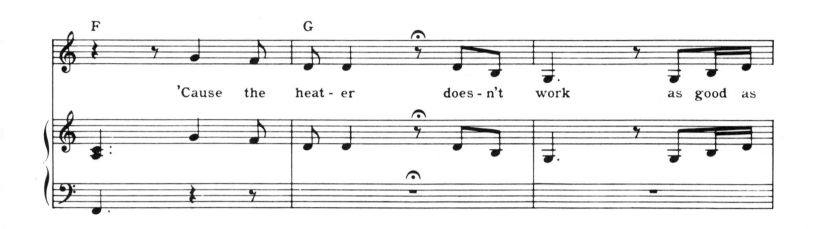

'Cause the heat - er does - n't work as good as

you.

(Ba - by come back.)

AND ALL THAT JAZZ
from CHICAGO

Words by FRED EBB
Music by JOHN KANDER

Copyright © 1973, 1975 by Unichappell Music Inc. and Kander-Ebb, Inc.
All Rights Administered by Unichappell Music Inc.
International Copyright Secured   All Rights Reserved

As If We Never Said Goodbye

from SUNSET BOULEVARD

Music by ANDREW LLOYD WEBBER
Lyrics by DON BLACK and CHRISTOPHER HAMPTON,
with contributions by AMY POWERS

© Copyright 1993 The Really Useful Group Ltd.
All Rights for the United States Controlled by Famous Music Corporation
International Copyright Secured   All Rights Reserved

al - ways._____ We'll have ear-ly morn-ing mad - ness,_____ we'll have

ma-gic in the mak - ing,_____ yes, ev-ery-thing's as if we ne - ver said good -

bye,_____ yes, ev-ery-thing's as if we ne - ver said good - bye._____

__ We taught the world new ways to dream.

BEAUTY AND THE BEAST
from Walt Disney's BEAUTY AND THE BEAST: THE BROADWAY MUSICAL

Lyrics by HOWARD ASHMAN
Music by ALAN MENKEN

© 1991 Walt Disney Music Company and Wonderland Music Company, Inc.
All Rights Reserved   Used by Permission

Big D
from THE MOST HAPPY FELLA

By FRANK LOESSER

Brightly

You're from Big D_____ I can guess_____ by the way you drawl_____ and the way you dress_____ You're from Big D, My, oh yes._____

© 1956 (Renewed) FRANK MUSIC CORP.
All Rights Reserved

BROTHERHOOD OF MAN
from HOW TO SUCCEED IN BUSINESS WITHOUT REALLY TRYING

By FRANK LOESSER

Handclapping Spiritual Feel

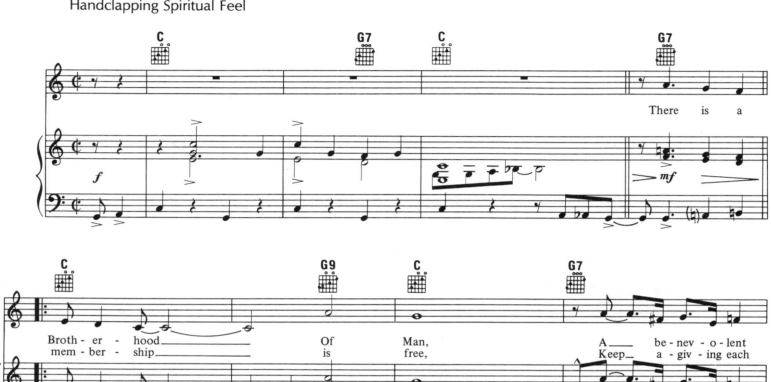

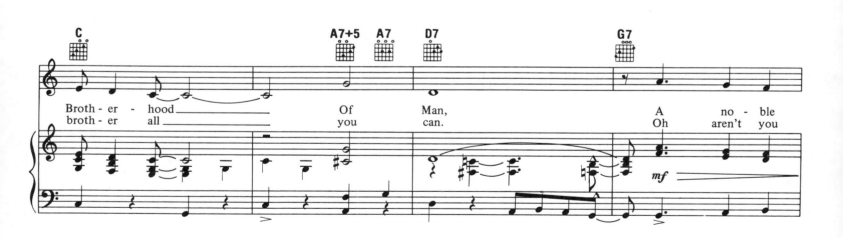

© 1961 (Renewed) FRANK MUSIC CORP.
All Rights Reserved

CABARET
from the Musical CABARET

Words by FRED EBB
Music by JOHN KANDER

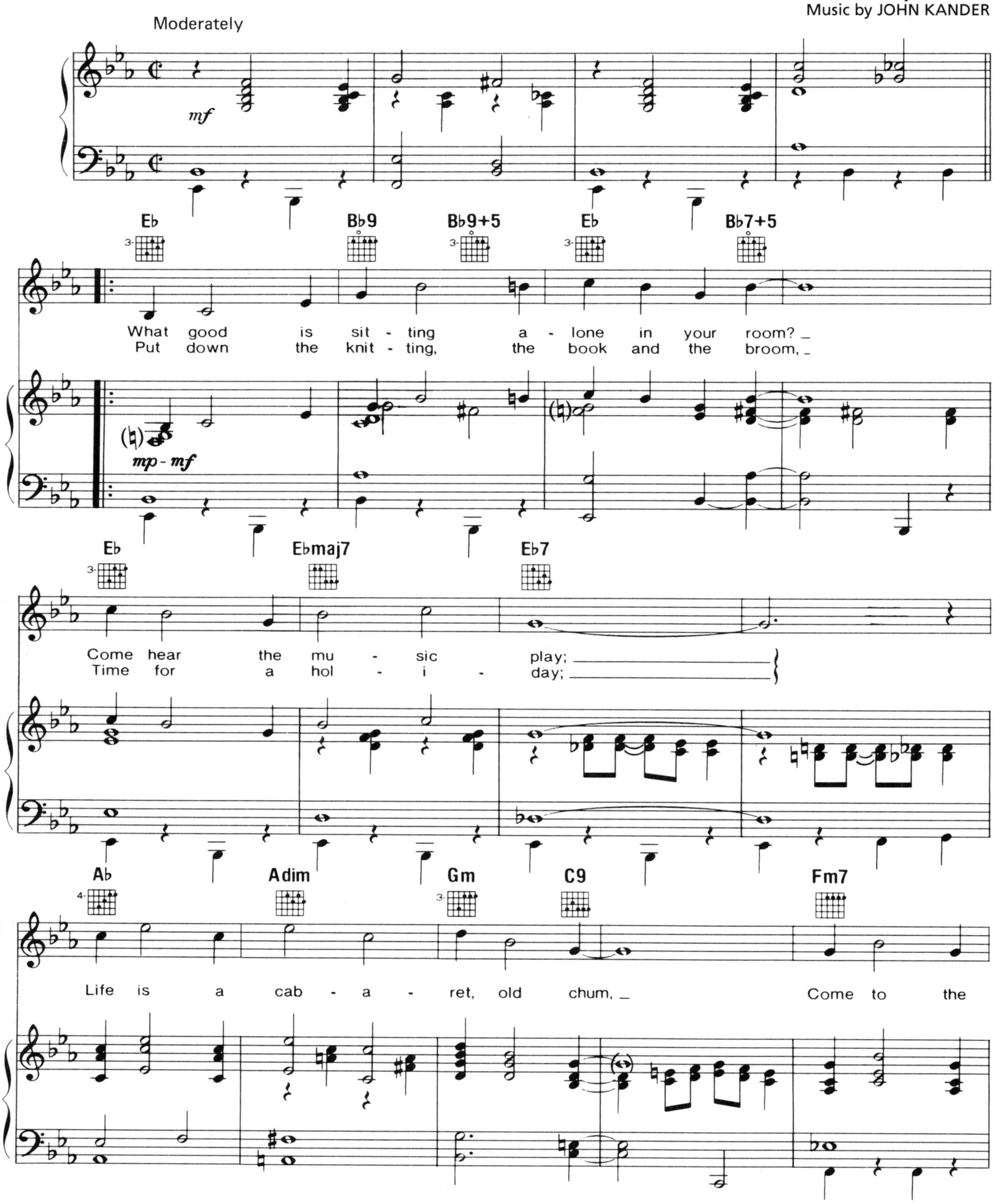
Moderately
mf
Eb
Bb9
Bb9+5
Eb
Bb7+5
What good is sit - ting a - lone in your room? _
Put down the knit - ting, the book and the broom, _
mp - mf
Eb
Ebmaj7
Eb7
Come hear the mu - sic play; ____
Time for a hol - i - day; ____
Ab
Adim
Gm
C9
Fm7
Life is a cab - a - ret, old chum, _ Come to the

Copyright © 1966, 1967 by Alley Music Corp. and Trio Music Co., Inc.
Copyright Renewed
International Copyright Secured All Rights Reserved
Used by Permission

COMEDY TONIGHT
from A FUNNY THING HAPPENED ON THE WAY TO THE FORUM

Words and Music by
STEPHEN SONDHEIM

Copyright © 1962 by Stephen Sondheim
Copyright Renewed
Burthen Music Company, Inc. owner of publication and allied rights throughout the World
Chappell & Co. Sole Selling Agent
International Copyright Secured   All Rights Reserved

EDELWEISS
from THE SOUND OF MUSIC

Lyrics by OSCAR HAMMERSTEIN II
Music by RICHARD RODGERS

Slowly

E - del - weiss, E - del - weiss, Ev - 'ry

morn - ing you greet me. Small and white,

Clean and bright, You look hap - py to meet

Copyright © 1959 by Richard Rodgers and Oscar Hammerstein II
Copyright Renewed
WILLIAMSON MUSIC owner of publication and allied rights throughout the world
International Copyright Secured   All Rights Reserved

EVERYBODY OUGHT TO HAVE A MAID

from A FUNNY THING HAPPENED ON THE WAY TO THE FORUM

Words and Music by
STEPHEN SONDHEIM

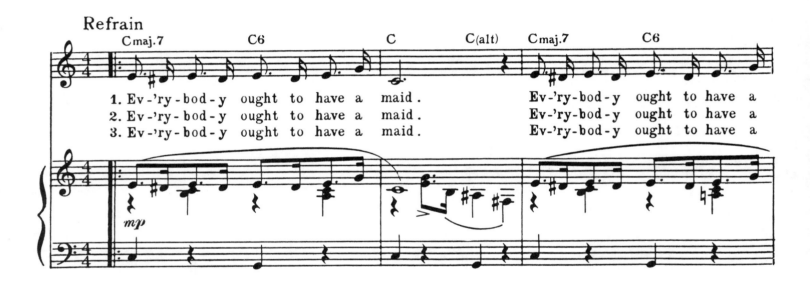

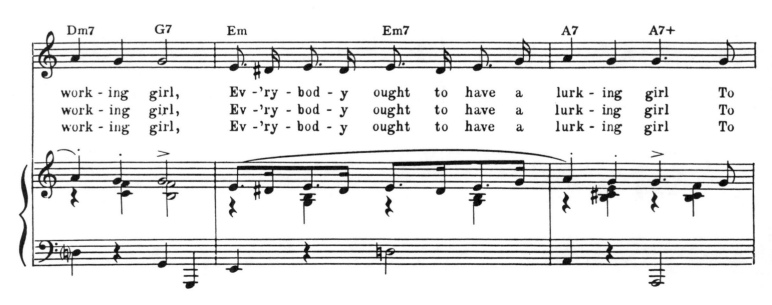

Copyright © 1962 by Stephen Sondheim
Copyright Renewed
Burthen Music Company, Inc., owner of publication and allied rights throughout the world
Chappell & Co., Sole Selling Agent
International Copyright Secured   All Rights Reserved

GODSPEED TITANIC
(Sail On)
from TITANIC

Music and Lyrics by
MAURY YESTON

Copyright © 1995 Yeston Music Ltd. (BMI)
Worldwide Rights Administered by Cherry River Music Co. (BMI)
International Copyright Secured All Rights Reserved

I BELIEVE IN YOU
from HOW TO SUCCEED IN BUSINESS WITHOUT REALLY TRYING

By FRANK LOESSER

© 1961 (Renewed) FRANK MUSIC CORP.
All Rights Reserved

GUYS AND DOLLS
from GUYS AND DOLLS

By FRANK LOESSER

© 1950 (Renewed) FRANK MUSIC CORP.
All Rights Reserved

HELLO, YOUNG LOVERS
from THE KING AND I

Lyrics by OSCAR HAMMERSTEIN II
Music by RICHARD RODGERS

Copyright © 1951 by Richard Rodgers and Oscar Hammerstein II
Copyright Renewed
WILLIAMSON MUSIC owner of publication and allied rights throughout the world
International Copyright Secured   All Rights Reserved

You fly down a street on a chance that you'll meet, and you
meet not real-ly by chance. _____ Don't
cry, young lov-ers, what-ev-er you do, don't cry be-
cause I'm a-lone. _____ All of my mem-'ries are

I WILL NEVER LEAVE YOU
from SIDE SHOW

Words by BILL RUSSELL
Music by HENRY KRIEGER

© 1994 MIROKU MUSIC (ASCAP)/Administered by A. Schroeder International Ltd., 200 West 51st Street, Suite 1009, New York, NY 10019 and
STILLBILL MUSIC (ASCAP), 1500 Broadway, Suite 2001, New York, NY 10036
International Copyright Secured All Rights Reserved

IF I CAN'T LOVE HER
from Walt Disney's BEAUTY AND THE BEAST: THE BROADWAY MUSICAL

Music by ALAN MENKEN
Lyrics by TIM RICE

Beast: And in my twist-ed face _____ there's not the slight-est trace _____ of an-y-thing that e - ven hints of kind - ness. And from my tor-tured shape, _____

© 1994 Wonderland Music Company, Inc., Menken Music, Trunksong Music Ltd. and Walt Disney Music Company
All Rights Reserved   Used by Permission

IF I LOVED YOU
from CAROUSEL

Lyrics by OSCAR HAMMERSTEIN II
Music by RICHARD RODGERS

Copyright © 1945 by WILLIAMSON MUSIC
Copyright Renewed
International Copyright Secured All Rights Reserved

KANSAS CITY
from SMOKEY JOE'S CAFE

Words and Music by JERRY LEIBER
and MIKE STOLLER

© 1959 (Renewed) JERRY LEIBER MUSIC, MIKE STOLLER MUSIC and NANCY NATHAN GOLDSTEIN
All Rights Reserved

crazy way of lovin' there and I'm gonna get me some.

I'm goin' to

They got a crazy way of lovin' there and

I'm gonna get me some.

THE LAST NIGHT OF THE WORLD
from MISS SAIGON

Music by CLAUDE-MICHEL SCHÖNBERG
Lyrics by RICHARD MALTBY JR. and ALAIN BOUBLIL
Adapted from original French Lyrics by ALAIN BOUBLIL

Music and Lyrics Copyright © 1987 by Alain Boublil Music Ltd. (ASCAP)
English Lyrics Copyright © 1988 by Alain Boublil Music Ltd. (ASCAP)
Additional Music and English Lyrics Copyright © 1989 and 1991 by Alain Boublil Music Ltd. (ASCAP)
Mechanical and Publication Rights for the U.S.A. Administered by Alain Boublil Music Ltd. (ASCAP)
c/o Stephen Tenenbaum & Co., Inc., 1775 Broadway, Suite 708, New York, NY 10019, Tel. (212) 246-7204, Fax (212) 246-7217
International Copyright Secured.   All Rights Reserved.   This music is copyright.   Photocopying is illegal.
All Performance Rights Restricted.

goes on and on. _____ Played on a

so - lo sax - o - phone, _____ it's tell - ing me _____ to

hold you tight _____ and dance like it's the last _____ night of the

world.

CHRIS: On the oth - er side of the earth_

LIVING IN THE SHADOWS
from VICTOR/VICTORIA

Words by LESLIE BRICUSSE
Music by FRANK WILDHORN

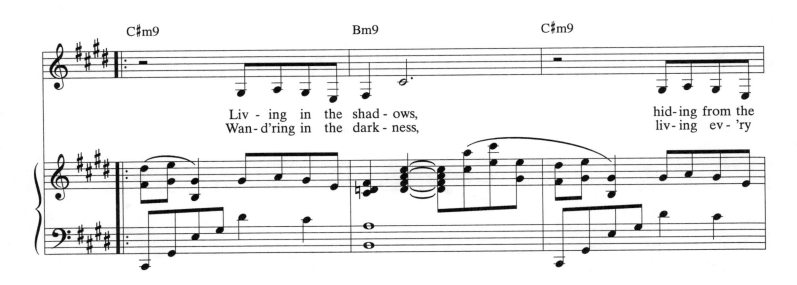

Liv - ing in the shad - ows,
Wan - d'ring in the dark - ness,

hid - ing from the
liv - ing ev - 'ry

Copyright © 1996 Stage & Screen Music Ltd. (BMI), Bronx Flash Music, Inc. (ASCAP), WB Music Corp. (ASCAP) and Scaramanga Music (ASCAP)
Stage & Screen Music Ltd. Administered by Cherry River Music Co. (BMI)
International Copyright Secured   All Rights Reserved
Used by Permission

sun - light,
mid - night,

hid - ing from the one light that
does-n't ev - er rid night that of

might help to guide you.
night - mares as love might.

Hid - ing from to -
Life is full of

mor - row,
dan - gers,

hid - ing from the day,
stran-gers ev - 'ry turn.

LAUGHING MATTERS
from Howard Crabtree's WHEN PIGS FLY

Music by DICK GALLAGHER
Lyrics by MARK WALDROP

Copyright © 1996 Punchu Music and Whatnot Music
All Rights Reserved   Used by Permission

LOVE CHANGES EVERYTHING
from ASPECTS OF LOVE

Music by ANDREW LLOYD WEBBER
Lyrics by DON BLACK and CHARLES HART

© Copyright 1988 The Really Useful Group Ltd.
All Rights for North America Controlled by R&H Music Co.
International Copyright Secured All Rights Reserved

Off _____ in-to the world we go, plan-ning fu-tures, shap-ing years.

Love _____ bursts in and sud-den-ly, all our wis-dom dis-ap-pears.

Love _____ makes fools of ev-ery-one: all the rules we make are

LOVE POTION NUMBER 9
from SMOKEY JOE'S CAFE

Words and Music by JERRY LEIBER
and MIKE STOLLER

© 1959 (Renewed) JERRY LEIBER MUSIC and MIKE STOLLER MUSIC
All Rights Reserved

MAKE BELIEVE
from SHOW BOAT

Lyrics by OSCAR HAMMERSTEIN II
Music by JEROME KERN

Copyright © 1927 PolyGram International Publishing, Inc.
Copyright Renewed
International Copyright Secured   All Rights Reserved

MORE I CANNOT WISH YOU
from GUYS AND DOLLS

By FRANK LOESSER

© 1949, 1950 (Renewed) FRANK MUSIC CORP.
All Rights Reserved

MY OWN BEST FRIEND
from CHICAGO

Words by FRED EBB
Music by JOHN KANDER

Copyright © 1973, 1975 by Unichappell Music Inc. and Kander-Ebb, Inc.
All Rights Administered by Unichappell Music Inc.
International Copyright Secured   All Rights Reserved

OL' MAN RIVER
from SHOW BOAT

Lyrics by OSCAR HAMMERSTEIN II
Music by JEROME KERN

Col-ored folks work on de Mis - sis - sip - pi, col-ored folks work while de white folks play. Pull - in' dose boats from de dawn to sun - set, git - tin' no rest till de judg - ment day. Don't look up an'

Copyright © 1927 PolyGram International Publishing, Inc.
Copyright Renewed
International Copyright Secured   All Rights Reserved

ON BROADWAY
from SMOKEY JOE'S CAFE

Words and Music by BARRY MANN, CYNTHIA WEIL,
MIKE STOLLER and JERRY LEIBER

© 1962, 1963 (Renewed 1990, 1991) SCREEN GEMS-EMI MUSIC INC.
All Rights Reserved   International Copyright Secured   Used by Permission

SEASONS OF LOVE
from RENT

Words and Music by
JONATHAN LARSON

© 1996 FINSTER & LUCY MUSIC LTD. CO.
All Rights Controlled and Administered by EMI APRIL MUSIC INC.
All Rights Reserved   International Copyright Secured   Used by Permission

SEEING IS BELIEVING
from ASPECTS OF LOVE

Music by ANDREW LLOYD WEBBER
Lyrics by DON BLACK and CHARLES HART

ALEX: See-ing is be-liev-ing, and in my arms I see her: she's
See-ing is be-liev-ing. I dreamt that it would be her: at

here, real-ly here, real-ly mine now— she seems at home here...
last life is here, full, life is fine now—

What-ev-er hap-pens, one thing is cer-tain: each time I see a

© Copyright 1989 The Really Useful Group Ltd.
All Rights for the US controlled by R&H Music Co.
International Copyright Secured All Rights Reserved

SHADOWLAND

Disney presents THE LION KING: THE BROADWAY MUSICAL

Music by HANS ZIMMER and LEBO M
Lyrics by MARK MANCINA and LEBO M

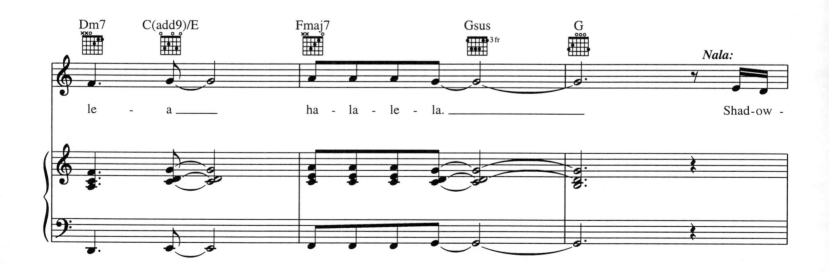

© 1997 Walt Disney Music Company and Wonderland Music Company, Inc.
All Rights Reserved   Used by Permission

SHALL WE DANCE?
from THE KING AND I

Lyrics by OSCAR HAMMERSTEIN II
Music by RICHARD RODGERS

Copyright © 1951 by Richard Rodgers and Oscar Hammerstein II
Copyright Renewed
WILLIAMSON MUSIC owner of publication and allied rights throughout the world
International Copyright Secured   All Rights Reserved

SOMEONE LIKE YOU
from JEKYLL & HYDE

Words by LESLIE BRICUSSE
Music by FRANK WILDHORN

Slowly, with expression

I peered through win-dows, watched life go by.
It's like you took my dreams, made each one real.
Dreamed of to-mor-row, You reached in-side of me

but stayed in-side. The past was hold-ing me,
and made me feel. And now I see a world

Copyright © 1990, 1995 Stage and Screen Music, Ltd. (BMI), Cherry Lane Music Publishing Company, Inc. (ASCAP),
DreamWorks Songs (ASCAP), Les Etoiles De La Musique (ASCAP) and Scaramanga Music, Inc. (ASCAP)
Worldwide rights for Stage and Screen Music, Ltd. administered by Cherry River Music Co. (BMI)
Worldwide rights for DreamWorks Songs, Les Etoiles De La Musique and Scaramanga Music, Inc. administered by Cherry Lane Music Publishing Company, Inc. (ASCAP)
International Copyright Secured   All Rights Reserved

heart's tak - en wing, _____ and I feel so a - live _____ 'cause
new way to live, _____ a _____ new way to love, _____ 'cause

some-one like you found me.

some - one like you found me. Oh, _____

some - one like you found some - one like me, and

THE SOUND OF MUSIC
from THE SOUND OF MUSIC

Lyrics by OSCAR HAMMERSTEIN II
Music by RICHARD RODGERS

The hills are a-live with the sound of mu - sic, ____

With songs they have sung for a thou - sand

years. ____ The hills fill my heart

Copyright © 1959 by Richard Rodgers and Oscar Hammerstein II
Copyright Renewed
WILLIAMSON MUSIC owner of publication and allied rights throughout the world
International Copyright Secured   All Rights Reserved

STANDING ON THE CORNER
from THE MOST HAPPY FELLA

By FRANK LOESSER

© 1956 (Renewed) FRANK MUSIC CORP.
All Rights Reserved

SUN AND MOON
from MISS SAIGON

Music by CLAUDE-MICHEL SCHÖNBERG
Lyrics by RICHARD MALTBY JR. and ALAIN BOUBLIL
Adapted from original French Lyrics by ALAIN BOUBLIL

Music and Lyrics Copyright © 1987 by Alain Boublil Music Ltd. (ASCAP)
English Lyrics Copyright © 1988 by Alain Boublil Music Ltd. (ASCAP)
Additional Music and English Lyrics Copyright © 1989 and 1991 by Alain Boublil Music Ltd. (ASCAP)
Mechanical and Publication Rights for the U.S.A. Administered by Alain Boublil Music Ltd. (ASCAP)
c/o Stephen Tenenbaum & Co., Inc., 1775 Broadway, Suite 708, New York, NY 10019, Tel. (212) 246-7204, Fax (212) 246-7217
International Copyright Secured. All Rights Reserved. This music is copyright. Photocopying is illegal.
All Performance Rights Restricted.

We have _ been blessed, you _ and I.

CHRIS: You are _ here like _ a mys - t'ry. _

I'm from _ a world that's _ so dif - f'rent _ from

all that _ you are. How in _ the

SUMMER NIGHTS
from GREASE

Lyric and Music by WARREN CASEY
and JIM JACOBS

© 1971, 1972 WARREN CASEY and JIM JACOBS
All Rights Controlled by EDWIN H. MORRIS & COMPANY, A Division of MPL Communications, Inc.
All Rights Reserved

THIS IS THE MOMENT

from JEKYLL & HYDE

Words by LESLIE BRICUSSE
Music by FRANK WILDHORN

Slowly

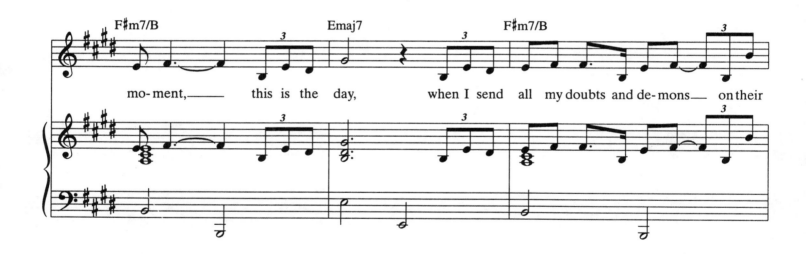

Copyright © 1990, 1995 Stage and Screen Music, Ltd. (BMI), Cherry Lane Music Publishing Company, Inc. (ASCAP),
DreamWorks Songs (ASCAP), Les Etoiles De La Musique (ASCAP) and Scaramanga Music, Inc. (ASCAP)
Worldwide rights for Stage and Screen Music, Ltd. administered by Cherry River Music Co. (BMI)
Worldwide rights for DreamWorks Songs, Les Etoiles De La Musique and Scaramanga Music, Inc. administered by Cherry Lane Music Publishing Company, Inc. (ASCAP)
International Copyright Secured   All Rights Reserved

WILLKOMMEN
from the Musical CABARET

Words by FRED EBB
Music by JOHN KANDER

Copyright © 1966 by Alley Music Corp. and Trio Music Co., Inc.
Copyright Renewed
International Copyright Secured   All Rights Reserved
Used by Permission

WITH ONE LOOK
from SUNSET BOULEVARD

Music by ANDREW LLOYD WEBBER
Lyrics by DON BLACK and CHRISTOPHER HAMPTON,
with contributions by AMY POWERS

Lento moderato

© Copyright 1993 The Really Useful Group Ltd.
All Rights for the United States Controlled by Famous Music Corporation
International Copyright Secured All Rights Reserved

WITHOUT YOU
from RENT

Words and Music by
JONATHAN LARSON

© 1996 FINSTER & LUCY MUSIC LTD. CO.
All Rights Controlled and Administered by EMI APRIL MUSIC INC.
All Rights Reserved   International Copyright Secured   Used by Permission

YOU SHOULD BE LOVED
from SIDE SHOW

Words by BILL RUSSELL
Music by HENRY KRIEGER

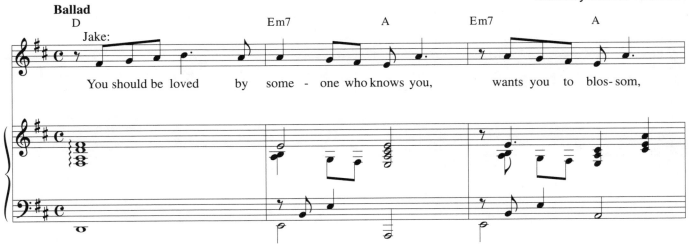

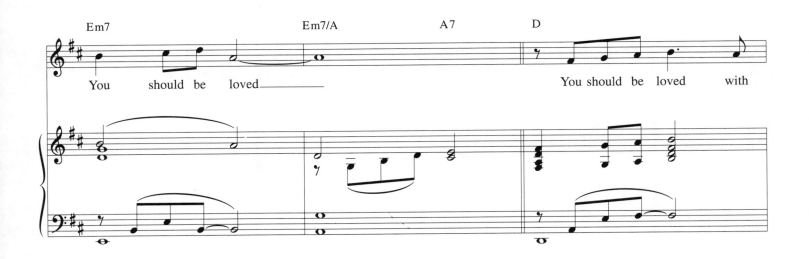

© 1994 MIROKU MUSIC (ASCAP)/Administered by A. Schroeder International Ltd., 200 West 51st Street, Suite 1009, New York, NY 10019 and
STILLBILL MUSIC (ASCAP), 1500 Broadway, Suite 2001, New York, NY 10036
International Copyright Secured   All Rights Reserved

YOU'LL NEVER WALK ALONE
from CAROUSEL

Lyrics by OSCAR HAMMERSTEIN II
Music by RICHARD RODGERS

Moderately

(with great warmth, like a hymn)

When you walk through a storm, hold your head up high And don't be a - fraid of the dark, At the end of the storm is a

Copyright © 1945 by WILLIAMSON MUSIC
Copyright Renewed
International Copyright Secured   All Rights Reserved